KT-434-631

FENG SHUI

FENG SHUI

Stephen Skinner

PARRAGON

About the Author

Stephen Skinner graduated in philosophy, geography and English from Sydney University. Having worked as a lecturer in geography he has brought to his research into feng-shui both the logical techniques of a geographer and an understanding of the mystical side of feng-shui. Time spent in the 1970s in Singapore and Hong Kong put him firmly in touch with modern practitioners of feng-shui who are consulted by even the largest building companies on projects ranging from new towns to office blocks and homes. He has carried out extensive field work and has worked on a number of feng-shui consultations in collaboration with Chinese feng-shui practitioners. His first book on feng-shui, *The Living Earth Manual of Feng-shui*, was written in 1976, long before the present interest in the subject, when almost all source material was in Chinese. He now works as a magazine publisher in London.

First published in 1999 by Parragon

Parragon
Queen Street House
4 Queen Street
Bath BA1 1HE UK

Copyringht © Parragon 1999

Originally designed and produced by Haldane Mason, London

Abridged, re-designed, packaged and produced by
Touchstone
Old Chapel Studio, Plain Road, Marden
Tonbridge, Kent TN12 9LS UK

Editor: Philip de Ste. Croix

ISBN 0-75253-237-5

Manufactured in China

Picture acknowledgements:
All photographs by Joff Lee, with the exception of the following:
Ace Photo Agency: page 55 (top)
Greg Evans International: page 25
The Garden Picture Library: page 62
Sally and Richard Greenhill: pages 48, 54
The Image Bank: pages 6, 13, 14, 27 (top, bottom right, bottom left, centre left), 30 (from second left to far right), 55 (bottom)
Rex Features Ltd: pages 7 (top right), 15, 27 (centre right), 30 (far left)
Trip Photographic Library: page 20
Michael Tse: page 10
Elizabeth Whiting & Associates: pages 56, 58, 60
Zefa Pictures: 7 (left), 27 (background)

Every effort has been made to trace the copyright holders and we apologize for any unintentional omissions. We would be pleased to insert the appropriate acknowledgement in subsequent editions of this publication.

Items which appear on pages 34 (top left) and 52 (top right) were kindly supplied by The Feng Shui Company, Ballard House, 37 Norway Street, London SE10 9DD.

Contents

> **Your feng-shui compass**
> **Please note that North is indicated by the
> direction of the red pointer**

Note: Remember that in all traditional feng-shui
illustrations (in line with Chinese practice) South is
always shown at the top of the page and North at
the bottom of the page. However North still means
the direction North, even in the Southern
Hemisphere. Feng-shui practitioners in Australia, for
example, should not reverse these directions simply
because of the different Hemisphere.

INTRODUCTION

The Art of
Feng-Shui

Feng-shui (pronounced 'foong-shway') is the ancient Chinese art of harnessing the heavens and the earth to bring health, wealth and good fortune by tuning in to the environment, seasonal changes, tides and vibrations of nature.

The principles of feng-shui are designed to alter your environment, your home and your heart, so that you feel at peace with yourself and the universe, and therefore able to use those changes in the tides of fortune that ceaselessly churn through your life to your best advantage.

Famous believers

The practice of feng-shui dates back thousands of years but it is still used today by many of the rich and famous who would not give it a second glance if they thought it was simply an ancient superstition. Even one of the most successful banks in the world today, the HSBC Group which owns the Midland Bank in the UK and has gone from strength to strength, had its head offices designed with advice from a feng-shui practitioner.

Lillian Too, the ex-managing director of the Grindlays Dao Heng bank in Hong Kong and the former deputy chairman of the billion-dollar company that owns Harvey Nichols, not only believes implicitly in feng-shui but is the best known writer on the subject.

Even the best relationships can benefit from direct feng-shui stimulation.

Feng-shui in the business world

It is no coincidence that in Hong Kong and Taiwan many of the buildings have feng-shui inspired features, and that these two states have amongst the highest per capita income in the world, closely followed in Asia by Singapore and Malaysia, two other advanced 'tiger' economies. Businessmen in these countries take feng-shui very seriously.

Richard Branson, one of the many successful business people who increasingly look to feng-shui to give them an extra edge.

Feng-shui is just as applicable in the work environment as it is in the home. After all we spend most of our life either in bed or work! It is important that the workspace environment is laid out in such a way that colleagues get on with each other, otherwise friction very easily develops.

Anyone familiar with the tycoons of the Far East will know that many of them regularly consult feng-shui masters in the course of their business, especially where it concerns property. It is well known for example that the owners of the Hyatt Hotel in Singapore have successfully used feng-shui advice to help increase their trade.

The Pa Kua is enhanced by the presence of the door guardian god. This particular one should be placed on the right-hand side of the door (looking inwards).

Feng-shui: the past and future

In the past the practice of feng-shui was limited to the Emperor of China and his family and functionaries. Ordinary people practised it on pain of death. However, you don't have to be an international bank, a huge corporation or a famous rock star to use feng-shui. This book will explain how even small changes in the feng-shui environment of your home can bring worthwhile benefits to the health, luck and happiness sectors of your life.

Don't expect feng-shui to help you win the lottery: it simply doesn't work like that. Feng-shui is not magic, but a natural practice. Undertaken correctly it will slowly but surely increase your feeling of rightness with the world; contentment will quickly replace dissatisfaction. Increasingly you will instinctively spend more time on things that bring you happiness and better fortune.

1 The Principles of Feng-Shui

Wind and Water

In Chinese *feng* means wind and *shui* means water. Between the immensity of heaven and the surface of the earth are clouds: these clouds consist of wind and water. The ancient Chinese saw wind and water as the intermediaries between heaven and earth. They thought that heaven directly affected their progress through life in a much more fundamental way than by simply creating changeable weather.

Clearly water is the sustainer of all life, whether plant, animal or human. Likewise, it is the wind which carries water from place to place, causes evaporation from the sea, and enables rain to fall on what would otherwise be parched land. Wind and water are therefore essential to our survival.

In addition, for a feng-shui practitioner these elements also carry the invisible life energy force *ch'i*. Therefore to ensure that there is an abundance of *ch'i* in a site or a home, it is important to observe the flow of wind and water and their interaction with the land.

The effects of *ch'i*

Ch'i acts on every level – on the human level it is the energy flowing through the acupuncture meridians or channels of the body (see pages 10-11); at the agricultural level it is the force which, if not stagnant, ensures fertile crops; and at the climatic level it is the energy carried on the wind and by the waters.

The mapping of these *ch'i* flows, and their deflection or enhancement, are the main principles of feng-shui. In other words, after mapping these *ch'i* flows, it is often necessary to correct, enhance or deflect them. For example, feng-shui practitioners maintain that just placing a small mirror or a wind-chime precisely in the correct place can sometimes make an enormous difference to your life. Instead of finding yourself always battling against life and your surroundings, whether in your love life or your career, you will find with the correct placement of some small feng-shui 'cure' that suddenly everything seems to go your way.

It is not easy to see why the placement of a mirror or even a change in the position of your bed should suddenly improve your relationships, but as you read through this book, you will begin to understand and to start experimenting with the simpler methods of feng-shui.

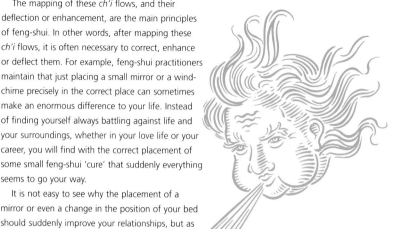

We live immersed in air, whose changing tides are the winds. Gentle breezes bring contentment while strong winds disperse life-enhancing ch'i.

The changing nature of flowing water not only symbolizes the theory behind feng-shui, but is actually one of the agents that carry the life-giving ch'i.

Feng-Shui and you

Don't interpret feng-shui as thinking superstitiously, but rather as thinking symbolically. Famous psychologists such as Carl Jung showed that the subconscious is impressed by symbols which the conscious mind might see as trivial. Although feng-shui actually works because of concentrations and dispersals of *ch'i*, if you find this difficult to accept you can always justify your feng-shui successes by reasoning that you have impressed your subconscious sufficiently for it to work on your behalf towards your desired ends.

Don't, however, make the mistake of thinking that feng-shui is arbitrary. You cannot just make up the rules as you go along. Sloppy and incorrect use of feng-shui can be just as effective in destroying your luck, as correct use can be in building it up.

Ch'i: *its Sources and Effects*

Ch'i is loosely referred to as 'cosmic breath' or 'life force', or more picturesquely the 'dragon's breath'. *Ch'i* flows through the human body and only departs on death, after which the body disintegrates. *Ch'i* is, therefore, literally 'the breath of life'.

The ability of the human body to perform almost superhuman feats, such as breaking bricks over the head as seen here, is increased by the accumulation of ch'i *in the body.*

Although not acknowledged by Western medicinal methods, acupuncture practitioners have long known of the existence of *ch'i*, and have built up elaborate maps of the 'meridians' or channels it uses to flow through the body. Acupuncture has been used to cure a number of medical conditions. Although acupuncture is widely accepted in the West as a valid form of therapy, there is still some progress to be made before the circulation of *ch'i* energy through the human body is accepted by Western science as an explanation of acupuncture.

Ch'i in the land

Ch'i also flows through and enlivens the earth, as well as the body. For example, according to feng-shui masters slow meandering rivers or streams accumulate *ch'i* in the land. This accumulation of *ch'i* strengthens both the body and the land. In short, through *feng* (wind or air) and *shui* (water) we can accumulate *ch'i*, which is beneficial to both man and his environment.

Accumulating *ch'i*

Those adept with the methods of internal alchemy or the martial arts have learned to accumulate *ch'i* in the body by a hard and exhausting regime, but for most of us the degree of passive absorption of *ch'i* from our surroundings, either at home or work, is the chief factor governing our energy and lucidity levels.

Living near or on concentrations of *ch'i* is reputed to be a source of greater concentration and clear headedness, abundant wealth, health and happiness. The Chinese see this as an accumulation of 'luck'. Luck, for the Chinese, is not something that just happens, it is something that can be worked at and consciously increased.

This brings us to the basic rules of *ch'i* accumulation, and hence also the basis of feng-shui. Straight lines or fast flowing streams or roads deplete and disperse *ch'i*, leading to the evaporation of luck. Stagnation contributes to the breakdown of *ch'i*, just as *ch'i* disperses when a body dies. The ideal conditions for accumulating *ch'i* are the slow, coiling, sinuous flow of water or wind which accumulate healthy *ch'i* in a suitably protected haven. This *ch'i* must be protected in order to accumulate, but it must also have access to another vigorous flow of *ch'i*, allowing the site to 'tap into a dragon vein', drawing off and hoarding *ch'i* successfully.

The rest of this book will look at how you can, with a bit of ingenuity, modify your home in order to attract and concentrate as much beneficial *ch'i* as possible. If you are buying a new home, then these rules may help you select a house or flat where you will be happier and more secure than if you had just purchased the first property that looked like good value.

A typical acupuncture chart such as may be found in practitioners' rooms across the world, showing the flow of ch'i *along meridians through the human body and various acupoints.*

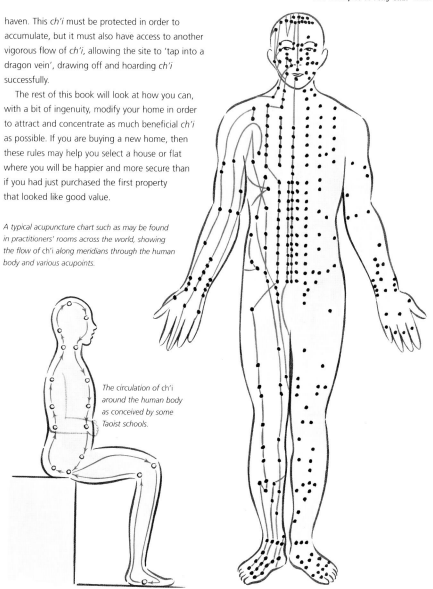

The circulation of ch'i *around the human body as conceived by some Taoist schools.*

Ch'i
in the Earth

At the very least the Chinese philosophers who considered *feng* (wind or air) and *shui* (water) to be the sustainers of mankind were good geographers and ecologists. However, they took their thinking much further. They understood that wind and water were not the only 'elements' flowing through the landscape and sustaining man. They perceived a more subtle energy flowing through the earth, and they called it *ch'i* or 'cosmic breath'.

Ch'i *flows in the land*
A classically good feng-shui site, nestled between two mountain ranges, with the ch'i *flows concentrated in the most sheltered part.*

The essence of feng-shui is to analyze a landscape, a town or a house to determine where the most favourable flows of *ch'i* are located, and how to produce new or enhance existing *ch'i* concentrations. The picturesque phrase for this is tapping the 'veins of the dragon'.

Wherever the 'cosmic breath' does not flow freely, stagnant *ch'i* will accumulate. On the other hand, *ch'i* must not be dispersed or buffeted by rough winds, for unprotected sites are unsuitable for the accumulation of *ch'i*. Naturally meandering watercourses halt and accumulate *ch'i*, but fast-flowing streams or those with long straight stretches cannot hold and accumulate their *ch'i* content.

The effects of good *ch'i*

Benign 'cosmic breath' is called *sheng ch'i*, and it brings with it well-being and a feeling of 'everything is right with the world'. Depleted stagnant 'cosmic breath' is called *sha ch'i*. Once your accumulating *ch'i* provides you with an increasingly positive attitude to the world, then it is just a short leap of imagination to see that your reaction to those around you is going to be more positive.

Detecting good and bad *ch'i*

A real feng-shui master will be able to sense the flows of *ch'i* in a site. For the rest of us, the flow of *ch'i* has to be deduced from rules or from signs. In a rural setting, animals will often follow lines of *ch'i* flow, and so sometimes paths worn by the tread of animals will trace out the lines of *ch'i*. In cities the flow of *ch'i* is often buffeted or contained by roads and man-made objects. Where these form sharp bends or straight paths, such as motorways or long stretches of telegraph poles, so the *ch'i* flows too rapidly and dangerously. However, those roads which curve, those lined by houses that do not confront each other and gardens which are planted according to feng-shui principles accumulate *ch'i* to the benefit of the occupants.

Water never flows naturally in a straight line. Here the meandering river has folded back on itself. A house positioned correctly in relation to this river will enjoy beneficial ch'i.

One step at a time

Feng-shui does not imply a lack of free will, it simply suggests that it is much easier to go with the flow rather than constantly struggle upstream against it. By careful manipulation of feng-shui techniques you can ensure that the flow is going your way. I say careful manipulation because it is necessary to progress slowly with feng-shui by making changes gradually, then allowing things to settle down for a week or so until you can judge whether things have improved as you planned.

If you rush into the deep end and make lots of immediate changes in your surroundings after reading this book, then you will never know for sure which changes have been beneficial and which have not. Worse than that, as a beginner you might make changes which have the reverse effect to the one desired and find that these cancel out the desired beneficial changes.

Lastly, by all means work carefully on your own feng-shui environment, but don't offer to change the feng-shui environment of friends, even with the best of intentions. Unless you are a fully trained feng-shui master or *hsein sheng,* let others make their own mistakes, rather than finding yourself responsible for some major reversal of their fortunes.

Energy Lines –
Avoiding 'Secret Arrows' and **Sha**

Everyone has days when nothing appears to go right, when it does not matter what you do, the results still turn out badly. A build-up in *sha ch'i* has the same effect, and brings with it lost opportunities, legal disputes and other misfortunes. Under such conditions it is impossible to make plans, or get your head 'above water' long enough to get out of the mess.

The long, straight road brings sha ch'i *rushing towards you, while the Eiffel Tower generates 'secret arrows'.*

*S*ha ch'i or 'killing breath' occurs when the *ch'i* flow is either stagnant or channelled in straight lines which become increasingly destructive forms of energy. *Ch'i* is similar to water in the same way as a gently flowing river is beneficial to transport and agriculture, while a raging torrent or a flash flood is deadly.

Ch'i flowing rapidly in straight lines is particularly dangerous. Modern cities are full of straight lines and therefore generate a lot of *sha ch'i*. It wasn't always so: most medieval European and pre-colonial Asian cities avoid the square grid street plans of modern city planners.

Sources of *sha* and 'secret arrows'

'Secret arrows' are straight lines which by virtue of their power to conduct *sha ch'i* pierce any accumulations of good *ch'i* and reduce their benefit. These lines can be formed by straight ridges, a row of roof-tops, railway embankments, telegraph wires or any set of parallel straight lines, and wherever these lines are directed or converge is subject to the

evil influence of these 'secret arrows'. Other examples of such 'secret arrows' include long straight roads leading directly away from the front door of a house, a row of electricity pylons, the pointed edges of large buildings, an overhead beam or a motorway flyover. Such 'secret arrows' can be effectively blocked off from a site or property by a wall, a row of trees or an embankment, or alternatively the 'secret arrows' may be deflected by the correct positioning of mirrors.

'Secret arrows' can be generated externally and be visible through a window or open door, or on a smaller scale they can form as a result of bad furniture placement within a room. Hence a priority with any feng-shui diagnosis is to check for any obvious 'secret arrows' and to establish whether they strike into your bedroom, at your office desk, your dining room or any area where you habitually spend significant amounts of time. In addition you should also open your front door, and standing on the threshold, check for any visible signs of poisonous 'secret arrows'.

The lines of traffic lights reveal the fast-flowing ch'i around the Arc de Triomphe in Paris.

Blocking 'secret arrows'

The elimination of 'secret arrows' takes precedence over any other feng-shui practice, and should be attended to foremost. The usual feng-shui 'cure' is to block out the offending sight. If the 'secret arrow' is aimed at the front door of your home, a particularly vulnerable spot, then try blocking the alignment with a hedge or try moving the entrance gate to the front garden to the left or right. If this is not practical, then hang a Pa Kua mirror (see page 53) over the door to relect the 'secret arrows' back to where they came from.

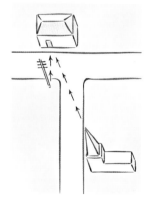

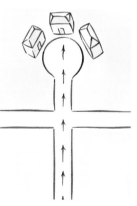

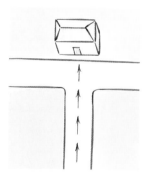

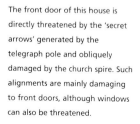

The front door of this house is directly threatened by the 'secret arrows' generated by the telegraph pole and obliquely damaged by the church spire. Such alignments are mainly damaging to front doors, although windows can also be threatened.

The house directly at the end of a straight cul-de-sac will be affected by 'secret arrows'. The other houses will, however, benefit from the pooling of *ch'i* at the end of the cul-de-sac.

A classic case of a road-generated 'secret arrow'. Try not to buy a house situated at the top of a T-junction, or in a position where a long, straight road 'strikes' the front door.

2 The Living Landscape

Earth, *Atmosphere and Heaven* Ch'i

The Chinese believe that there are three kinds of luck: the luck you make yourself *(ren choy)*; the gifts that are bestowed upon you by heaven at birth *(t'ien choy)*; and the benefits that come from your environment or 'earth luck' *(ti choy)*. You cannot easily affect your 'heaven luck', but you can affect your 'earth luck'.

The five types of Weather ch'i extend between Heaven ch'i and Earth ch'i.

The ridges and lines in the landscape form the body, veins and pulse of the Earth 'dragon' while streams, pools and underground watercourses are thought to be the dragon's blood. The veins and watercourses both carry *ch'i*, the life-force in the earth. Lines of trees, roads and even railways also carry or disperse *ch'i* across the landscape. The geometry of the flow of *ch'i* can be amazingly complex, forming a lattice or a network between the main 'dragon veins', for no part of the earth is dead.

In this book we are concerned with the laws that govern *ti choy* 'earth luck'. How you take advantage of that luck *(ren choy)* is up to you. *Ch'i* pervades both Heaven and Earth and the space in between, so *ch'i* is divided into:

Earth *ch'i (ti ch'i)* or host *ch'i*

This is contained in the 'dragon veins' of the earth. It runs through the earth and along its watercourses and is subject to decay. It is governed by the Later Heaven Sequence of the Trigrams.

Heaven *ch'i (t'ien ch'i)* or guest *ch'i*

This is affected by the heavens and may overrule the effect of Earth *ch'i*. It is governed by the Earlier Heaven Sequence of Trigrams.

Weather *ch'i*

There are five types of weather *ch'i* which mediate between Earth and Heaven *ch'i* and which are carried in the rain, sunshine, heat, cold and wind. These are the moveable *ch'i*, the fluctuating elements distributed between the more fixed *ch'i* of Heaven and Earth, and they are a mixture of the nature of both Heaven and Earth. They are subject to decay like the Earth *ch'i*.

Ideal feng-shui conditions

The essence of good feng-shui is to trap the *ch'i* energy flowing through the site and accumulate it without allowing it to go stagnant. The second consideration is to ensure that the *ch'i* is not dispersed.

One of the feng-shui classics, *Han Lung Ching*, says that *ch'i* rides the winds and disperses, meaning that windy, unprotected sites will lose any accumulated *ch'i*. However, when bounded by slow-flowing water the *ch'i* actually halts. Here again are the two elements of feng-shui, wind and water. The wind, if tamed to a gentle breeze, will bring with it the circulating *ch'i*, while if the water follows a curved pattern and is appropriately oriented it will keep the *ch'i* in the site, so increasing its physical and spiritual fertility.

The third consideration is not to allow the *ch'i* to become torpid or stagnant in which case it becomes *ssu ch'i* or stagnant *ch'i*. If the site is completely hemmed in so that the air does not circulate or the water nearby is sluggish and stagnant, the ground

A stylized view of the five-clawed Imperial dragon.

literally gives off damp and stinking exhalations *(sha)*, rendering the place unfit from a feng-shui point of view. *Sha* is the antithesis of *ch'i* and can be translated as 'noxious vapour'. It is sometimes called *sha ch'i* or *feng sha* (noxious wind).

If these three conditions can be achieved through the natural configuration of the landform, then an excellent house site has been discovered.

The feng-shui expert looks for the dragon hidden in the landscape.

The **Living Water** of Rivers

If the watercourses near a property or site run straight and rapidly, the *ch'i* is scattered and wasted before it can serve any beneficial purpose. Those places where the *ch'i* is enclosed to the right and left and has a drainage system carrying off the water in a sinuous course are the best for accumulating *ch'i*.

Chinese dragons were considered to be water creatures, living in rivers or clouds, and not fire-breathing monsters like Western dragons.

Charting *ch'i*

Watercourses are the most obvious flowlines of *ch'i*. In fact the Chinese word for stream actually sounds like *ch'i*. The general rule is that water that flows too quickly or in straight lines conducts *ch'i* away from a spot rapidly, and is therefore undesirable; and that slow, sinuous, deep watercourses, on the other hand, are conducive to the accumulation of *ch'i*, especially if they form a pool in front of the property under consideration.

In an urban environment we have to interpret roads in the same light as streams, but with the proviso that as most roads are straight they are more likely to produce damaging 'secret arrows' rather than healthy *ch'i*.

Aiding *ch'i*

The landscape can be significantly altered by man to improve feng-shui. Man-made bends can be put in straight river stretches or sharp bends can be made more rounded. Even artificial confluences of rivers or streams can be created. Preferably the house should be nestled amongst tributaries of the river rather than directly on the main or trunk watercourse, especially if it runs too fast to accumulate *ch'i*. The more tributaries in the stream, the more potent the *ch'i* accumulation.

A stream flowing from the East or the West is auspicious if it flows directly towards the house, deflects around it, and then meanders away. This is because the *ch'i* brought by the stream enters the house directly (by the straight stretch of water) but is taken away from the house indirectly: it therefore accumulates. If possible the stream leaving the site should be out of sight of the house, so that there is no visible loss of the *ch'i* accumulated.

The Living Landscape

Dragon points

As a curved and meandering course is the best indication of *ch'i*, so the junction of two watercourses is a key dragon point. If the feng-shui practitioner is using a compass, this junction will be a significant and easily aligned siting point.

The junction should form a graceful curve rather than a harsh bend and the watercourse formed should harmoniously cross and re-cross the area in front of the property to enhance positive flows of *ch'i*.

Stream confluences are beneficial because of the concentration of *ch'i*, while the branching of a stream flowing through coarse sediment or at the delta of a river is dispersive of *ch'i*. Sharp bends, like straight lines, are unfavourable as they act like 'secret arrows' destroying or removing the ch'i accumulations. Curves in the watercourse are much more conductive as they mimic the naturally sinuous shape of a 'dragon'.

Positive river locations

Positive river locations include those where the rivers 'embrace' the house or site in a protective fashion.

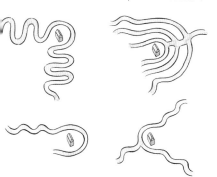

These formations rejoice in very poetic Chinese names, such as 'Warrior pulls bow' (top right) or the 'Coiled dragon' (top left).

River patterns & sites

Various real and fantastic river patterns: the more complex patterns were sometimes artificially created by Chinese hydraulic engineers. The red dot shows a potential *ch'i* accumulating site for a house.

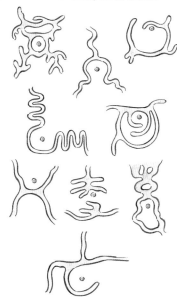

Negative river locations

Sharp bends, straight river stretches and houses or sites 'squeezed' in a sharp V or Y do not accumulate beneficial *ch'i*.

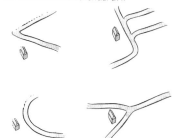

Mountains *and* Dragon Bones

Symbolically, the landscape betrays the presence of *ch'i* in its shape. To an advanced practitioner of feng-shui,

the flows of *ch'i* beneath the surface of the landscape are as obvious as the *ch'i* flow strength or weakness detected in the body by an acupuncturist.

The extraordinary mountains of southern China, where the five Element types of mountains are easily picked out.

C*h'i* is symbolized in its positive (Yang) form as a dragon, and in its negative (Yin) form as a tiger (see also pages 26-27). The two different *ch'i* currents in the Earth's crust, the one male (positive), the other female (negative), are called, respectively, the green dragon and the white tiger. Looking South, the green dragon should always be positioned to the left (East), and the white tiger to the right (West) of any site. The very best site is where the two *ch'i* currents cross or copulate.

The perfect feng-shui location

A perfect site forms a complete horseshoe shape. Such a formation of hills or mountains is the sure sign of 'the presence of a true dragon'. Obviously we can't all live in idyllic countryside settings, but we can use this ideal to model changes in our present home.

An illustration of this ideal is the favourable situation of the city of Canton (see illustration), which is set in the angle formed by two chains of hills running in gentle curves towards each other, forming a complete horseshoe.

If these dragon-tiger symbols cannot be perfectly found in the site then the generalized conjunction of 'male' and 'female' ground will do almost as well. Boldly rising elevations are Yang (male), while uneven, softly undulating ground is called Yin (female) ground. In areas where such characteristics are not obvious, other features such as tall buildings can take the place of the dragon mountain range, while structures at a lower height symbolize the tiger.

As a consequence of the above set of rules, it is apparent that flat land is not propitious from a feng-shui point of view. In fact where flat land surrounds a house, then walls, artificial mounds of earth or lines of trees are often incorporated to the North to improve *ch'i* accumulation qualities.

The traditionally-shaped plan of Canton faces South on to the river, and is embraced by artificially extended canals and surrounded by supportive hills to the North. Several protective pagodas were built inside the Northern wall.

Mountains

These are the traditional abodes of the immortals, of dragons and gods. Mountains are the pristine source of Yang *ch'i* flows, the most virile and powerful landscape feature and therefore a fit lair for dragons. Rocky outcrops are sometimes seen as dragon bones. It is, therefore, one of the first requirements of a feng-shui practitioner that he should be able to tell at a moment's glance which star, Planet and Element is represented by any given mountain. The five types of mountain, and the Elements and Planets with which each is associated, are illustrated (right).

The five mountain types

The five Elements (and Planets) and the shape of their associated mountain forms:

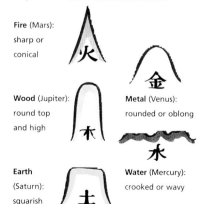

Fire (Mars): sharp or conical 火

Wood (Jupiter): round top and high 木

Earth (Saturn): squarish 土

Metal (Venus): rounded or oblong 金

Water (Mercury): crooked or wavy 水

The **Four** Directions, **Four** Celestial Animals and **Four** Seasons

The green dragon and white tiger locked in an embrace. The best location for a house is the point where they symbolically join or copulate.

The most basic Directions are the four compass points North, South, East and West. To simplify remembering the qualities of each Direction, feng-shui practice attributes a symbolic animal to each point.

In the Northern Hemisphere, the greatest heat of high summer comes from the South, the direction of the sun at midday. Therefore the Element Fire and the season of Summer are attributed to the South and identified with the similarly coloured red raven or crimson phoenix, the mythical bird which rises from the ashes of the fire, like the sun rises each day from night. The beneficial feng-shui feature to look for to the South is a low 'footstool' hill or, in an urban environment, a low wall.

North

The cold dark North, by contrast, is attributed to Water, whose symbolic animals include the black tortoise or the warrior, and whose season is Winter. In the landforms surrounding a site, this Direction is most auspicious if occupied by a background of encircling hills, trees, or in an urban environment, a level of higher buildings.

East and West

To the East, where the sun rises, is Spring with the azure or green dragon as its symbolic creature. Its Element is Wood. Opposite in the West is Autumn symbolized by the white tiger. Its Element is metal. The complementary pairing of the green dragon and the white tiger are considered by feng-shui practitioners to be very important.

For the feng-shui to be good, buildings or mountains flanking a site to the West and East must have some hint of the characteristics of these two animals. The perfect location, the point where most *ch'i* is accumulated, is supposed to be where the dragon and tiger meet or near the green dragon's genitals.

Centre of the compass

Finally, the fifth Element, Earth is sited at the centre of the compass, acting as a point of balance for the other four. The wind which circulates between them is not considered to be an Element, even though the Ancient Greeks counted Air as one of the Elements.

The Four Seasons

The sun rises in the East, just as the year begins in Spring; reaches its peak in the South (Mid-Summer); sets in the West (Autumn); and is dark in the North (Mid-Winter).

> **Spring** – East
> **Summer** – South (maximum Yang)
> **Autumn** – West
> **Winter** – North (maximum Yin)

North and South

Remember that in all traditional feng-shui illustrations (in line with Chinese practice) South is always shown at the top of the page and North at the bottom of the page. However North still means the direction north, even in the Southern Hemisphere. Feng-shui practitioners in Australia, for example, should not reverse these directions because they live in a different Hemisphere.

Four celestial animals

A stylized view of the four celestial animals in relationship to the compass Directions. The front of the house faces the red phoenix in the South and is backed by the black tortoise of the North.

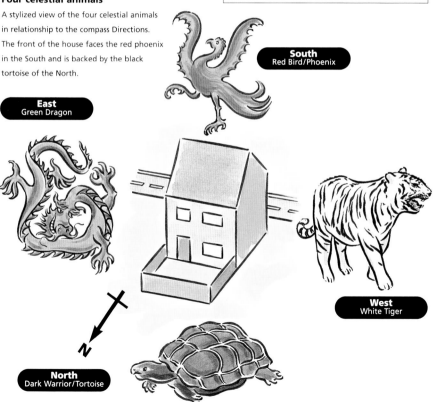

South
Red Bird/Phoenix

East
Green Dragon

West
White Tiger

North
Dark Warrior/Tortoise

Feng-Shui

The **White** *Tiger and* *the* **Green Dragon** *in the* Landscape

By locating surrounding landscape features or buildings that fit the symbolic requirements of a good site, and by visualizing the four celestial animals embodied in the physical representations, the feng-shui practitioner helps to connect the site with the beneficial influences of the four celestial animals, which offer the occupants of the site their protection.

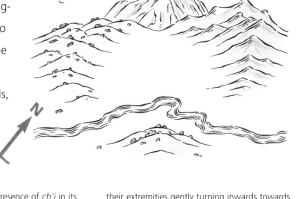

The ideal site, or Hsueh, is at the rear of the lowland facing the river and small knoll in the foreground. The high mountain to the North backs the site and the green dragon and white tiger flank it. Note that the green dragon hills are slightly higher than the white tiger range of hills.

The landscape betrays the presence of *ch'i* in its positive (Yang) form as a dragon, and in its negative (Yin) form as a tiger. The two different *ch'i* currents in the earth's crust, the one male (positive), the other female (negative), are called, respectively, the green dragon and the white tiger. Facing South, the green dragon must always be to the left (East), and the white tiger to the right (West) of any site. The site is most beneficially placed when the surrounding hills form a horseshoe, that is to say where two ridges of hills starting from one point run out to the right and left in a graceful curve,

their extremities gently turning inwards towards each other, one slightly longer than the other. Such a formation of hills or mountains is said to be the sure indicator of a true dragon. Of course in urban areas these hills are replaced by high or low adjoining buildings, each representing the four celestial animals.

The landscape and the city

The feng-shui practitioner looks very precisely at the landscape surrounding a site for a hint of the symbolic presence of the celestial animal forms. For example,

in a good site it should be possible to look to the East and see a range of mountains or hills representing a recumbent dragon. Then upon looking to the West, the practitioner hopes to see a lower range of hills symbolizing the white tiger. He/she then looks to the North of the site to find a range of hills that act as a 'backing' to the site, symbolizing the tortoise. Finally he will be delighted at what he finds if there is a very low 'footstool'-shaped mound to the South symbolizing the phoenix.

In a built-up city, the dragon and the tiger forms are much harder to see. It may simply be that another house to the East will represent the dragon, while a lower one to the West will embody the tiger. A low wall to the front, signifying the red phoenix, is often easier to find.

Buildings in a city have to make use of other structures to represent the support of the tortoise mountain. The World Trade Center in New York provides this backing for the rest of Manhattan. Note, however, that the communications mast will also generate 'secret arrows'.

In most cases, the landscape does not form a perfect horseshoe or 'armchair'-shaped surround for the site, but then very few sites are perfect. Feng-shui practitioners who are called in to diagnose the site of a grave will often suggest building a backing made from bricks or concrete behind the grave to protect it from the malign influences of the North. Chinese armchair graves, such as the one above, are very ornate.

3 The Direction-Finding Art

Yin *and* **Yang**

Yin and Yang are at the root of the Chinese view of the universe. At a simple level they are the female and male principles respectively, wife and husband, woman and man, dark and light, sour and sweet. At a more universal level they are negative and positive.

Ch'ien:

The Heaven Trigram *Ch'ien* is made up of three Yang (unbroken) lines. This Trigram is completely Yang.

In Chinese philosophy, life is conceived as a mixture of light and dark, warmness and coolness. The ideal is the proper mixture, in the right proportions. The Yin-Yang symbol (see illustration) is the perfect example. At the centre of the cosmological system is unity or *wu-chi* symbolized by a circle. This develops into *t'ai-chi* which is sometimes shown as three alternating rings of dark and light, or in more modern times the Yin-Yang symbol. The middle of the light half (Yang) contains a seed of dark (Yin), and the dark half (Yin) contains a seed of light (Yang). The trick is to obtain a life-giving and sustaining balance.

Applied to the landscape, the hills represent Yang while the valleys symbolize Yin. Yang also applies to the sunny side of mountains, while Yin symbolizes the darker North-facing slopes.

Yin and Yang are represented in the Chinese classic text, the *I Ching*, as a whole line (Yang) and a broken line (Yin). As the whole line is in one part and the broken line is made up of two parts, Yang is equated with the number one and Yin with the number two: it follows that all odd numbers are Yang and all even numbers are Yin. Odd numbers are associated with creation (Yang) and even

K'un:

The Earth Trigram *K'un* is made up of three Yin (broken) lines. This Trigram is completely Yin.

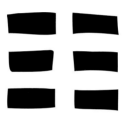

numbers with nourishing and completion (Yin). From a feng-shui point of view Yin implies the fertile shady North side of a hill, while Yang is the warm impregnating Southern side.

Yin governs the Earth and all that is negative, female, dark, water, soft, cold, deadly or still; while Yang derives from Heaven and all that is positive, male, light, fiery, hard, warm, living and moving. The combination and permutation of the Yang and the Yin forms the rest of the universe whose life and breath is *ch'i*.

The two breaths of nature, or types of *ch'i*, are essentially one breath. They make up the male and female principles: when they unite they constitute the beginning or birth of things; when they disperse they cause decay, dissolution and death.

Yin and Yang interact with each other to produce the next level of complexity, the five Elements: Water, Fire, Wood, Metal and Earth. From these Elements come what Taoists call 'the ten thousand myriad things' or the rest of creation.

Wood

Water

Fire

Metal

Earth

The Trigrams

From the Yin and the Yang are derived the eight Trigrams (see pages 28-29), each of which is made up of three lines on top of one another, each line being either whole (Yang) or broken (Yin). Of these

Trigrams the male all-Yang Trigram, made of three whole lines, is called *Ch'ien* or Heaven, while the *K'un* all-Yin Trigram is made up of three broken lines and represents Earth. The other six Trigrams are made up of a mixture of both Yin and Yang.

The **Eight** *Ancient* Trigrams

The positive and negative qualities of Yin and Yang are expressed as either a solid line (Yang) or a broken line (Yin). These lines taken three at a time provide eight possible combinations of Yin and Yang which are known as the eight Trigrams.

It is said that the sage Fu Hsi invented the Trigrams more than 4000 years ago. Later King Wen (c. 1150 BC) combined each of the eight Trigrams with each of the others to produce 64 hexagrams. Each of these hexagrams had a textual interpretation added to it, first by the Duke of Chou and later by Confucius, forming the Chinese classic book the *I Ching* (also known as the *Classic of Changes*). This book is central to the Chinese view of the universe and is also used as an instrument of divination. It is said that all changes can be predicted from these 64 hexagrams.

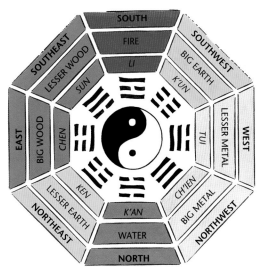

Sites and houses

When considering the site of a property or home, the Trigrams are laid out in the Later Heaven Sequence (see diagram opposite and pages 32-33), with the Trigram *Li* facing South. The Trigrams are used to evaluate watercourse entry and exit points. In other words, the feng-shui compass is used to determine the sector in which a stream or pond first becomes visible, and the sector from which it finally drains away out of sight. The Trigrams also illustrate the qualities which may be associated with each source of water *ch'i* and how it will affect the site.

The Pa Kua

The Pa Kua is an octagonal-shaped symbol which contains the four cardinal Directions and the four intercardinal Directions of the compass, plus the Elements and the Trigrams. Fire is opposite to Water. The two Trigrams attributed to Earth are opposite each other, with *K'un* being the stronger Yin Earth Trigram. Both pairs of Wood and Metal Trigrams are adjacent to each other. *Ch'ien* being all Yang is obviously the stronger of the two Metal Trigrams.

The Trigrams

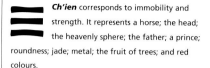 **Ch'ien** corresponds to immobility and strength. It represents a horse; the head; the heavenly sphere; the father; a prince; roundness; jade; metal; the fruit of trees; and red colours.

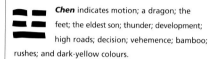 **Chen** indicates motion; a dragon; the feet; the eldest son; thunder; development; high roads; decision; vehemence; bamboo; rushes; and dark-yellow colours.

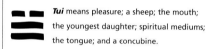 **Tui** means pleasure; a sheep; the mouth; the youngest daughter; spiritual mediums; the tongue; and a concubine.

 **K'an** signifies peril; a pig; the ears; the middle son; channels and streams; hidden things; a bow; a wheel; anxiety; pain in the ears; high spirits; a drooping head; thieves; strong trees; and the colour blood-red.

K'un represents docility; bovine cattle; the belly; the mother; Mother Earth; cloth; cauldrons; parsimony; large carts; figures; a multitude; a handle; and the colour black.

Sun means penetration; a fowl; the thighs; the eldest daughter; wood; wind; length; height; a backwards and forwards motion; bald-headedness; a broad forehead; and the colour white.

Ken indicates stoppage; a dog; the hands; the youngest son; paths and roads; small rocks; gates; fruits and cucumbers; porters or eunuchs; finger rings; rats; and birds with large bills.

Li means beauty; brightness; a pheasant, the bird of the South in the Later Heaven Sequence; eyes; the middle daughter; the sun; lightning; helmets; spears and swords; dryness; crabs; spiral uni-valves; and mussels.

Inside the home

The Trigrams provide indications of the best rooms for specific purposes or for specific members of the family. As each Trigram is associated with one or other family member, so he/she is better placed if his/her bedroom is located in the corresponding sector of the house, or one which does not conflict with his/her Trigram.

For feng-shui the significance of, for example, the relationship between the Trigrams and family members is of vital importance when considering which member of a family will receive the most benefit by having his or her representative Trigram aligned with the main door of the house.

A traditional view of the sage Fu Hsi as a mountain, an indication of the intimate relationship between the Trigrams he invented and the feng-shui landscape.

Using the **Five Elements**

The Five Elements, Fire, Water, Wood, Metal and Earth, evolve out of Yin and Yang. By Elements the Chinese meant the principal energies behind the manifest physical universe. The Element Wood, therefore, is not the same as a chunk of timber, but is the animating principle that dwells in any forest or vegetation.

The Chinese term for the Elements is *hsing*, which indicates movement, so perhaps 'the five moving agents' might be a more appropriate name for them. This term reinforces the concept that the Elements generate and destroy each other in a continuous cycle. Like the Trigrams and hexagrams of the *I Ching*, these are symbols of change and transformation, and can be used to improve the feng-shui of your home.

All the Elements are related to and interact with each other. Wood represents the essence of all vegetation, which is fed by Water, which covers and binds the Earth, which is cut down by Metal

implements, which ignite to give Fire. Water is understood to be all forms of fluid including the liquefaction of Metal within the Earth. Earth is understood to mean all mixed, impure and inanimate substances including the ash produced by Fire.

The relationship between the five Elements and the Directions of the compass is important for the practice of feng-shui, and the knowledge of how each Element relates to the others helps to solve practical feng-shui problems. The colours of the Elements relate to interior decoration and suggest how certain Elements and their effects can be stimulated by using colour.

The qualities of the five Elements

	fire	**water**	**wood**	**metal**	**earth**
COLOUR	Red	Black/Dark Blue	Green	White/Gold	Yellow/Brown
SEASON	Summer	Winter	Spring	Autumn	—
DIRECTION	South	North	East	West	Centre

The Elements and you

On a personal level each of us has an Element associated with our year of birth (see box). If you are born in an Earth year then it will be very sensible to surround your home with things which are symbolic of Earth, or even better the Element which generates Earth (see The Production Cycle, page 35). As Fire creates Earth it would be a good Element to emphasize. Wood on the other hand destroys Earth (see The Destruction Cycle, page 35) and would not be a good Element to emphasize in your home. If you are a Fire person, then a Water-oriented environment might not be the best as Water destroys Fire.

In addition, everyone has an Element associated with their month, day and hour of birth. Taken with the year, this gives the eight character Elemental make-up of the individual, the basis of a Chinese horoscope. But the Element of the year of birth is the most important in a feng-shui context.

How to work out your Element

To check the	Element of Birth Year	
Element of your	0	Metal
year of birth, keep	1	Metal
subtracting 10 from	2	Water
the last two digits	3	Water
of your year of	4	Wood
birth until you	5	Wood
reach a number	6	Fire
which is 10 or less,	7	Fire
then read your	8	Earth
Element off from	9	Earth
the table:	10	Metal

Table of Elements, Trigrams, animals, emblems and seasons

TRIGRAM		ELEMENT	ASSOCIATED ANIMAL	EMBLEM	ASSOCIATED SEASON	INTERPRETATION
☰	Ch'ien	Metal	Dragon, Horse	Heaven	Late Autumn	Creative; strength; roundness; vitality
☷	K'un	Earth	Mare, Ox	Earth	Late Summer-Early Autumn	Receptive; yielding; nourishment
☳	Chen	Wood	Galloping Horse, Flying Dragon	Thunder	Spring	Movement; arousal
☵	K'an	Water	Pig	Moon and Water	Mid-Winter	Curved objects; flowing water; danger
☶	Ken	Lesser Earth	Dog, Rat, Black-billed Birds	Mountain	Early Spring	Steadiness; stillness; gates; fruits; seeds
☴	Sun	Lesser Wood	Hen	Wind	Early Summer	Gentleness; penetration; growth; vegetative growth
☲	Li	Fire	Pheasant, Toad, Crab, Snail, Tortoise	Sun and Lightning	Summer	Adherence; dependence; weapons; drought; brightness
☱	Tui	Lesser Metal	Sheep	Lake and Seawater	Mid-Autumn	Joy; serenity; reflections, mirror images

風
水 Feng-Shui

The **Eight Pa Kua** *Directions*

The Pa Kua is the basic tool of Compass
School feng-shui. It is an eight-sided
figure, which allocates each
of the eight Trigrams to the
eight compass Directions,
to the four cardinal
points of the compass
and to the four
intercardinal points.

FAME

SOUTH · FIRE · LI

WEALTH · SOUTHEAST · LESSER WOOD · SUN

MARRIAGE · SOUTHWEST · BIG EARTH · K'UN

FAMILY · EAST · BIG WOOD · CHEN

CHILDREN · WEST · LESSER METAL · TUI

KNOWLEDGE · NORTHEAST · LESSER EARTH · KEN

K'AN

HELPFUL PEOPLE · NORTHWEST · BIG METAL · CH'IEN

WATER

CAREER · NORTH

The Later Heaven Sequence

The Pa Kua in the Later Heaven
Sequence (see box) shows which
Trigram is allocated to which compass
point. These Pa Kua directions are very versatile.
They can be applied either to a whole city, to a
whole house or its garden, or a flat in a house or
just to a room in a flat. It is effective at each of
these levels because it determines Directions and a
Direction is the same whether viewed from a single
room in the smallest flat or from the walls of a
whole city.

The Pa Kua and your home

By placing the Pa Kua symbol over a plan of your
home you can divide it up into eight sectors, North,
South, East, West, Southwest, Southeast, Northwest
and Northeast. The eight sectors of the Pa Kua
correspond to an aspect of your life.

*The key to the Pa Kua: the correlation between the compass
Directions, Trigrams, life aspirations, Elements and colours.*

Now we begin to connect the apparently abstract
Chinese symbols with your home and aspirations. By
orientating the top of the Pa Kua to the South
compass Direction of the plan of your home, office
or room you get eight even sectors, each related to
a different facet of your life. In an L-shaped house
or flat, one or more of the Pa Kua sectors will be
missing.

The Direction-Finding Art

The two arrangements of the Pa Kua

There are two traditional orders in which the Trigrams are assigned to the compass points. These two arrangements are called the Earlier Heaven Sequence and the Later Heaven Sequence.

The difference between these is that the Earlier Heaven Sequence is the ancient or ideal heavenly order and is used mainly in the feng-shui of tombs or grave sites. It has *Ch'ien* or the Heaven/Father Trigram located in the South opposite to *K'un* or the Earth/Mother Trigram located in the North. These Trigrams are exact opposites of each other, as are the Fire (East) and Water (West) Trigrams of the other axis.

This arrangement is highly symmetrical, and the Northwest/Southeast and Southwest/Northeast Trigram pairs are also exact opposites.

Unfortunately this arrangement of Trigrams for the dwelling places of the living is less perfect, and so the Later Heaven Sequence devised by King Wen, which is appropriate to the feng-shui of houses and gardens, is used instead. Most feng-shui books give both sequences, which is very confusing. We will only use the Later Heaven Sequence in this book as this is the one needed for determining home and town feng-shui.

Earlier Heaven Sequence

Later Heaven Sequence

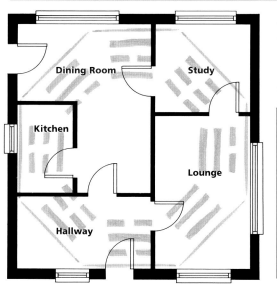

The Pa Kua on this home plan shows the Trigram *K'un* in the Southwest study, *Chen* in the East-facing kitchen and *K'an* at the North-facing front door.

The Pa Kua sectors

The eight sectors of the Pa Kua each correspond to a life aspiration

South	fame
Southwest	marital happiness and relationships
West	children
Northwest	new beginnings and mentors
North	career prospects
Northeast	education
East	family relationships and health
Southeast	wealth and prosperity

33

Production and Destruction of the **Five Elements**

The five Elements are connected together in two cycles. The first, the Production Cycle, explains which Element generates the next and the second, the Destruction Cycle, demonstrates which Element destroys another. These cycles are one of the most important keys to the practice of feng-shui as they offer practical guidance on how to improve your personal feng-shui.

The Production Cycle works like this: Wood burns to produce Fire, which results in ash (or Earth) in which Metal may be found. Metal is also found in the veins of the earth from which (according to Chinese thought) sprang the underground streams (Water) which nourish vegetation and produce Wood.

Each Element destroys another in the Destruction Cycle shown, so that in feng-shui theory the destroyer is hostile to the destroyed Element.

These cycles are important not just as theory, but because they provide the key to enhancing or modifying the feng-shui of your home. The rule is that to enhance a sector you add to its corresponding Element, and to stimulate this Element you add the Element that produces it. For example, assume that you want to stimulate your wealth sector. From the Pa Kua it is apparent that the sector of your home associated with wealth is the Southeast and that this sector is associated with the Element of Wood (see the diagram on page 32).

Looking at the Production Cycle you can see that the Element that produces Wood is Water. Therefore the addition of a Water feature, such as a fish tank or a small fountain, in the Southeast sector will strengthen Wood in that quarter and thus stimulate wealth luck and prosperity. That is how the Production Cycle can work to your advantage. If, on the other hand, you installed a Metal feature in the Southeast sector, then you would destroy the Element of Wood in this sector (see the Destruction Cycle, opposite), reducing your chances of increasing your wealth.

The Destruction Cycle

This cycle is a little more tricky to use. Metal cuts down and destroys Wood. Wood draws its essence from and destroys Earth. Earth in turn destroys Water. Water extinguishes and destroys Fire. Fire melts and destroys Metal, which brings us back to the beginning of the Destruction Cycle.

Using this cycle you could minimize the effects of a particular Element by symbolically adding the Element that destroys it. For example, an overabundance of Fire in one sector of the house could be reduced by adding a Water feature, as Water destroys Fire. There is a more subtle way of achieving this end by using the Element that is produced by the Element you are seeking to reduce. Thus applying Earth to a sector will reduce an overabundance of the Element Fire (see Production Cycle right).

The cycles of the elements

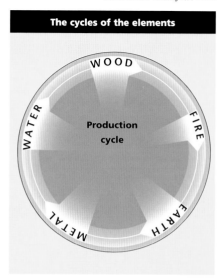

The Production Cycle can be used to boost or stimulate the next Element around the Cycle.

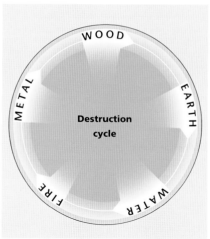

The Destruction Cycle can be used to reduce or modify Elements by using the destroying Element in the cycle.

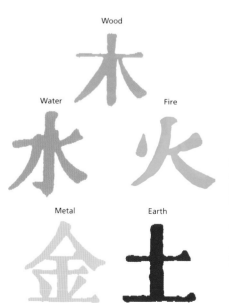

Wood

Water

Fire

Metal

Earth

The Lo Shu *Magic Square*

The Lo Shu is one of the most ancient tools of feng-shui. The
Lo Shu is a magic square with a 3 x 3 grid of nine chambers
which helps the feng-shui practitioner to analyze a house or
flat, and predict flux and changes for its occupants.

The Lo Shu square is a 'magic' square because
the numbers placed in its nine chambers add up
to 15 regardless of which direction you add them
up, even diagonally. The numbers in the Lo Shu are
used in many feng-shui formulae.

What does it do?

The Lo Shu neatly coincides with the eight Trigrams
arranged in the Later Heaven Sequence of the Pa
Kua, plus a central chamber which is assigned to
Earth. The chamber which contains the number 9
is aligned with the South and the number 1 with
the North.

The Lo Shu is used extensively in Compass School
feng-shui. It is used like the Pa Kua to divide up the
house into nine sectors, or it can be used on a
smaller scale to divide a room into nine sectors.

The Eras of the Lo Shu

One of the secrets of the Lo Shu is that it unlocks
the time dimension for feng-shui, and allows
practitioners to decide precisely when is the best
time to make changes to the site, the home or the
interior decoration.

In drawing up a feng-shui analysis of a house,
the original Lo Shu may be used, but the order of
the numbers is modified over time. Time is divided

into Eras of 60 years, consisting of three cycles of
20 years. During each cycle the order of numbers
differs from the original Lo Shu. The current cycle
began in 1984 and will end in 2003. For the
duration of this cycle, every house built during this
time will have a 7 at the centre of its Lo Shu, with
the other numbers moved around in a specific order
(see The Current Lo Shu). However the basic pattern
is all we need to know.

The numbers change in the Lo Shu in a logical
manner from Era to Era. If you connect up the nine
chambers in numeric order, you get a diagram
which shows the order in which the numbers move
from Era to Era (see The Pattern of Numbers).

Compass School: *Wang Chih*

Not until the rise of the Sung dynasty were all the
elements of feng-shui gathered into one methodical
system which combined every form of influence that
heaven and earth were supposed to have on human
affairs. The Directions and Positions School or
Compass School is also referred to as the Fukien
School of feng-shui. This School places great stress
on the Pa Kua, the eight Trigrams, the Heavenly
Stems and Earthly Branches and the Constellations,
assigning a place of minor importance to the
landscape configurations of the earth.

The Lo Shu square around the world

As well as in China, the Lo Shu square has been part of the magical traditions of the Middle East and Europe for at least 2000 years. In Western magic derived from ancient Hebrew traditions, a square with exactly the same numbers is known as the square of the planet Saturn and under some circumstances also as the square of the Earth. In the West there are seven planetary squares and they were used to generate the signs which were used to control the spirits of the planets. The zig-zag arrow pattern is the seal of Saturn or Earth.

Adding the numbers together vertically equals 15

Adding the numbers together horizontally equals 15

Adding the numbers together diagonally equals 15

The original Lo Shu

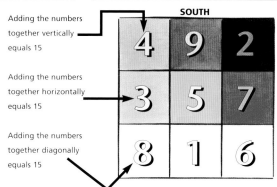

SOUTH

The archetypal Lo Shu arrangement of the numbers 1 to 9. There are eight different ways of adding them together, each of which produces 15. The 24 Directions (see pages 40-41) multiplied by 15 give the 360° measurement of the circle.

The current Lo Shu

SOUTH

6	2	4
5	7	9
1	3	8

In each period the numbers 'fly' around the Lo Shu. During the cycle from 1984 to 2003 the numbers reside in the Lo Shu squares as illustrated. The number 7 falls in the centre and is therefore called the reigning number.

The pattern of numbers

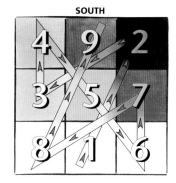

SOUTH

If you join the numbers from 1 to 9 sequentially, the arrows trace out a pattern that resembles the ancient square of Saturn or Earth in Western occult tradition. The numbers move or 'fly' around the Lo Shu following the order indicated by the arrows.

The **Ten** Heavenly Stems and **Twelve** Earthly Branches

The Ten Heavenly Stems and Twelve Earthly Branches are key categories in feng-shui, the Chinese calendar and cosmology. The Stems and Branches are used to measure time and direction.

The Ten Heavenly Stems		
NUMBER	**NAME**	**ELEMENT**
1	甲 chia	Wood
2	乙 i	
3	丙 ping	Fire
4	丁 ting	
5	午 wu	Earth
6	己 chi	
7	庚 keng	Metal
8	辛 hsin	
9	壬 jen	Water
10	癸 kuei	

The relative luck of the Stems is related to their association with the Trigrams. The unlucky Stems 1, 2, 9 and 10 are associated with the *Ch'ien* and *K'un* Trigrams which are not propitious because they are overwhelmingly Yang and Yin respectively, with no mixture or balance. On the other hand, because Stems 3, 4, 7 and 8 are associated with the *Ken* and *Sun* Trigrams which have a suitable mixture of Yin and Yang, they are considered to be lucky.

Stems 1 and 9 are seen as Yang 'orphans', that is, children left alone in the world who therefore need to extend their own self-reliance in a very Yang way.

Stems 2 and 10 symbolize Yin emptiness: quite the reverse of stems 1 and 9, but again an undesirable state, with no balance asserting itself. Orphanemptiness literally means 'unlucky' in Chinese.

Stems 3 and 7 represent Yang prosperity – again a lucky blend. 'Prosperity-assistance' is the Chinese compound word for 'lucky'.

Stems 5 and 6 represent the centre and do not partake of any particular Direction, nor are they allocated a Trigram. The Stems also stand for the numerals from 1 to 10 or, if grouped in Yin-Yang

pairs, they represent the five Elements, each being either a 'big' or 'lesser' version of each Element.

The Twelve Earthly Branches

The Twelve Earthly Branches give specific information about time and place. The twelve main points on the compass are those allocated to the Twelve Earthly Branches and their basic function is to mark the Directions. Taken on their own the Branches also indicate the twelve two-hour divisions of the day as well as the twelve months of the year. A year, a month and an hour can all be designated by one of the Twelve Earthly Branches, which can then in turn signify a Direction of the compass for each of these times.

The seasons fit in naturally with the Branches and indicate the best times of the year for initiating projects connected with building or buying. The water solstice occurs halfway through Branch *tzu* (due North) which is the beginning of the Chinese New Year, and the rest of the Branches follow in order assigning the parts of the compass to the time of the year.

The Twelve Earthly Branches

The Twelve Earthly Branches with their associated
Directions, Roman numbers and 'zodiacal' animal.
Note that the Branches and Stems are combined
on pages 40-41 to form the full
24 Directions of the
feng-shui compass.

SOUTH
VII
WU

VI
SSU

VIII
WEI

V
CHEN

IX
SHEN

IV
MAO

WEST
X
YU

III
YIN

XI
HSU

II
CHOU

XII
HAI

I
TZU

NORTH

Snake · Horse · Goat
Dragon · · Monkey
Rabbit · · Cock
Tiger · · Dog
Ox · · Pig
· Rat ·

The **24** Compass Directions

The most basic division of the *lo p'an* or feng-shui compass is by the eight Trigrams. Then the eight Trigrams are sub-divided into 24 compass Directions, three Directions for each cardinal point North, South, East and West, and three Directions for each intercardinal point, Southwest, Northwest, Southeast and Northeast.

Each of the 24 compass Directions is classed as either Yin or Yang. Rather confusingly these 24 compass Directions are also made up of three other sets of symbols:

- Twelve Earthly Branches
- Eight of the Ten Heavenly Stems
- Four of the Eight Trigrams

However, this is not as complicated as it sounds, as four Trigrams mark the intercardinal points, and four Branches mark the cardinal points. The two missing Heavenly Stems are reserved for the Element of Earth at the centre of the compass.

These 24 Directions are the key to the feng-shui compass. It also contains the 24 Directions that appear on Chinese mariners' compasses. Most feng-shui compasses feature the ring of 24 Directions three times. It is not necessary to remember the Chinese name of each Direction, but understanding its qualities helps with further feng-shui analysis.

The 24 Directions

Each of the eight cardinal and intercardinal points is printed in bold type in the table (right). Each of the four intercardinal points, Southwest, Southeast, Northwest and Northeast, retains its own Trigram from the Later Heaven Sequence (see pages 32-33). These four Trigrams are flanked on either side by one of the Earthly Branches. Each of the cardinal points also take a Branch, flanked on either side by a Heavenly Stem.

If you look at the fourth column of the table above you can see that three Yang Directions alternate with three Yin Directions. Also if you ignore the four Trigrams, the Earthly Branches alternate with the Heavenly Stems. These 24 compass Directions become important when we come to look at the orientation of a house, and which of these 24 Directions it faces.

For precision readings with a Western compass, the corresponding degrees are also listed in the table. Thus, if a particular mountain top is visible at 146°, we would be able to tell from the table that the corresponding Yang Branch in the Southeast sector is *Ssu*.

This is one of the most important illustrations in the book because it ties together all of the Compass School symbology you have learned up to now. On the outside, it first shows the whole circle divided up into Yin and Yang sectors. The next ring shows the points of the compass. The four 'corner points', Northwest, Southwest, Southeast and Southwest, each have one of the Trigrams attributed to it. The rest of the 24 Compass Directions have either a Branch or Stem attributed to them.

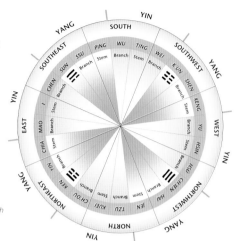

The 24 Directions of the compass are as follows:

DIRECTION	CHINESE NAME	WHAT IT IS	YIN OR YANG	RANGE OF COMPASS DEGREES	CHINESE CHARACTER
	Ping	Stem	Yang	157.5-172.5	
South	**Wu**	**Branch**	**Yin**	**172.5-187.5**	丙 午 丁
	Ting	Stem	Yin	187.5-202.5	
	Wei	Branch	Yin	202.5-217.5	
Southwest	**K'un**	**Trigram**	**Yang**	**217.5-232.5**	未 坤 申
	Shen	Branch	Yang	232.5-247.5	
	Keng	Stem	Yang	247.5-262.5	
West	**Yu**	**Branch**	**Yin**	**262.5-277.5**	庚 酉 辛
	Hsin	Stem	Yin	277.5-292.5	
	Hsu	Branch	Yin	292.5-307.5	
Northwest	**Ch'ien**	**Trigram**	**Yang**	**307.5-322.5**	戌 乾 亥
	Hai	Branch	Yang	322.5-337.5	
	Jen	Stem	Yang	337.5-352.5	
North	**Tzu**	**Branch**	**Yin**	**352.5-7.5**	壬 子 癸
	Kuei	Stem	Yin	7.5-22.5	
	Ch'ou	Branch	Yin	22.5-37.5	
Northeast	**Ken**	**Trigram**	**Yang**	**37.5-52.5**	丑 艮 寅
	Yin	Branch	Yang	52.5-67.5	
	Chia	Stem	Yang	67.5-82.5	
East	**Mao**	**Branch**	**Yin**	**82.5-97.5**	辛 辛 乙
	I	Stem	Yin	97.5-112.5	
	Chen	Branch	Yin	112.5-127.5	
Southeast	**Sun**	**Trigram**	**Yang**	**127.5-142.5**	辰 巽 巳
	Ssu	Branch	Yang	142.5-157.5	

A Simple **Feng-Shui Compass**

A full *lo p'an*

A seventeen-ring nineteenth-century lo p'an showing how complex a full feng-shui compass can be.

After using Form School or landscape feng-shui to evaluate the surroundings of the site, the next step is to use a feng-shui compass. The compass was not necessarily first used in China as a navigational instrument. It may well have been used to determine the direction of the earth's magnetic field, or even for feng-shui purposes.

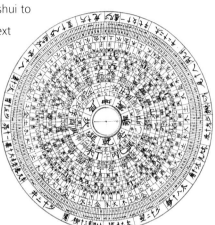

A full *lo p'an*

A seventeen-ring nineteenth-century lo p'an showing how complex a full feng-shui compass can be.

The feng-shui compass is called a *lo p'an* and it is much more complex than a Western maritime compass. *Lo p'ans* are obtainable through specialist feng-shui shops.

A full feng-shui compass

The compass is in a way an extension of the Pa Kua circle of Trigrams. A full feng-shui compass can have as many as 36 rings with between eight and 365 divisions on each ring. They are usually made of wood and fit into a square wooden base. In the centre of the circular disc is a glass-covered depression called the Heaven Pool containing the magnetic needle, painted so that it points to the South (or a small circle at the end of the needle should be lined up with two small dots on the floor of the Heaven Pool which indicate magnetic North). A North-South line is drawn on the floor of the Heaven Pool. When the needle is exactly aligned with this line, with the red end pointing South, then the compass is correctly aligned.

A simple feng-shui compass

The inner ring of a simple *lo p'an* is divided up into the eight Trigrams. The next couple of rings are combinations of the Elements, the numbers of the Lo Shu Magic Square and the 24 compass Directions. The inner rings of the compass are the ones of immediate interest to us, as they relate to Yang feng-shui, that of houses and cities. The middle and outer rings are more concerned with Yin feng-shui, the feng-shui of graves.

The *lo p'an* and your home

To assess the feng-shui qualities of your home, or any site, the first step is to identify each of the compass Directions. To do this you need a compass. This does not have to be a feng-shui *lo p'an*; it can be any conventional compass.

Applied Compass Feng-Shui

First use the compass to check for South, remembering that we are talking about the Direction in which a compass points not map South which is approximately 7.5 degrees different from the magnetic compass bearing.

The square base into which the compass is set has two precisely aligned cross hairs intersecting at right angles. These cross hairs are used to indicate the reading on the rings.

A traditional Ch'ing dynasty compass made of wood showing how the disc fits into the base.

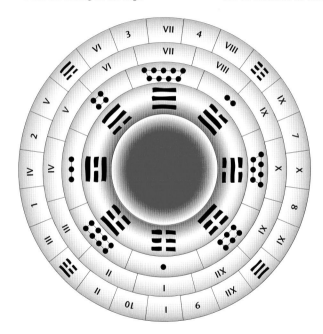

Lo P'an

A basic *lo p'an* should have the following seven rings:

0   Heaven Pool – the actual compass needle and well.

1   The eight Trigrams arranged in the Earlier Heaven Sequence.

2   Eight of the nine numbers of the Lo Shu Magic Square are represented symbolically, so that 1 is represented by one dot, 2 by two dots connected by a line, and so on. As 5 applies to the centre it is not represented in this circle.

3   The Twelve Earthly Branches.

4   The 24 Directions of the Chinese compass, made up of Branches, Stems and Trigrams.

5   The 24 *Chieh ch'i* or fortnightly divisions of the Solar calendar.

6   The 60 Dragons or Sexagenary characters, namely the five Heavenly Stems matched with the Twelve Earthly Branches.

7   The 28 unevenly spaced *hsiu* or Chinese constellations.

The inner four rings of a typical *lo p'an*

In contrast to the full seventeen-ring lo p'an compass shown on the opposite page, the box to the right explains the seven rings in a basic lo p'an. The most important inner four rings are analyzed graphically above. The Earthly Branches are shown as Roman numerals and the Heavenly Stems as ordinary numbers, while the Trigrams appear in their usual form.

43

Using the **Feng-Shui** *Compass*

The first reading to be taken with the compass is to determine the direction that the front door of the house faces: this is called the Facing Direction. The opposite direction to this is known as the Mountain or Siting Direction and it is 180° from the Facing Direction.

A Western hiking compass which enables you to take a siting on a specific landform feature, and read off the exact number of degrees to establish its bearing.

The 24 Directions of the compass are shown on page 41. To take a reading of the Facing Direction, position yourself just inside your open front door looking outwards. The procedure differs slightly depending upon the equipment used, as explained next.

A traditional *lo p'an*
There are several steps to using a traditional *lo p'an*. First the outer square base should be lined up parallel with the front door, so that one of the cross hairs points out of the door at right angles to the threshold. Then the inner circular disc should be rotated until the magnetic needle lines up with the line underneath it. Usually the small circle at one end of the needle should be aligned with the two red dots on the floor of the Heaven Pool. It is important to line the needle up precisely. Then the cross hair pointing out of the front door will indicate the Facing Direction.

A homemade *lo p'an*
A *lo p'an* can be made from a cardboard ring with the 24 Directions marked upon it with a hiking compass mounted in the middle. First turn the compass until the north-pointing needle indicates North. Then turn the cardboard ring until the centre of Direction *tzu* (see page 41) also lines up with North. Then sight from the centre of the compass in the Facing Direction.

A Western hiking compass
Use a hiking compass with a sight which reads exact numbers of degrees. Remember that 0° (also 360°) is North, 90° is East, 180° is South and 270° is West. Stand inside the doorway, as far back as possible, and sight directly out of the front door. Read off the degrees, then look up the table on page 41 to determine which of the 24 Directions is the Facing Direction. Each of the 24 Directions occupies 15°. Due magnetic North lies exactly in the centre of the Direction *tzu*. (Map North is not relevant).

Facing and Mountain Directions
Having identified the Facing Direction write it down in the box provided. Then the direction 180° away that is pointing in exactly the opposite direction, known as the Mountain or Siting Direction, can also

The compass directions applied to a house

Applying the basic four rings of the compass to this house plan, the Facing Direction pointing straight out of the front door is Earthly Branch VII or *Wu*. This means that the Mountain Direction is directly opposite, the Earthly Branch I or *Tzu*.

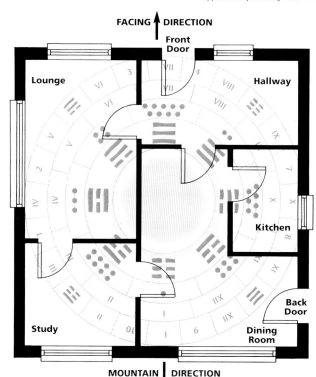

FACING DIRECTION

Front Door

Lounge

Hallway

Kitchen

Back Door

Study

Dining Room

MOUNTAIN DIRECTION

be read off. This pair of Directions, the Facing Direction and the Mountain Direction, are the characteristic Directions of the house.

Occasionally a building obviously faces a different Direction from that of its front door. For example, a flat might not have a front door which faces in the same Direction as the front door to the whole block. In this instance both Directions should be checked. If you live in a flat and the front door of the building faces in a different Direction, or if the Facing Direction of your house is not the same as its front-door Direction, you will need to take a second reading which will give you a second Facing and Mountain Direction.

A modern feng-shui compass from the author's collection.

Workpoint

Enter here the Directions of your front door:

	Degrees	One of the 24 Directions
Facing Direction		
Mountain Direction		

Calculating your
Personal Magic Number

To find your personal lucky and unlucky Directions, you must first calculate your own 'Kua number'. Technically this is the 'natal star' for your year of birth and part of Chinese Nine House Astrology.

Traditional feng-shui books provide tables and complicated calculations for deducing your Kua number, but the following explanation is a short cut.

Working out your Kua number

The formula for calculating your Kua number differs according to whether you are a man or a woman. You should work out your Kua number and that of your partner.

First you must establish your year of birth according to the Chinese calendar. In practice this step only affects those who were born between 1st January and 20th February. If you were born in this part of the year before the Chinese New Year, you should subtract one from your year of birth (see box). If you were not born in January or early February, you simply ignore this step.

If you are a man, start the calculation by adding together the last two digits of the year of your birth. (If the total number is greater than 9, then add the two digits of the total number together). This will give you a single digit. Subtract this digit from 10. This is your Kua number.

The calculation for women is slightly more complicated than for men. If you are a woman, begin by adding together the last two digits of the year of your birth. If the total number is greater than 9, then add the two digits of the total number together to give you a single digit. Add 5 to this digit. (If the total number is greater than 9, then add the two digits of the total number together.) The result is your Kua number.

Good and bad Directions

Once you have calculated your Kua number then look at the illustration of the Pa Kua (opposite page) for this number and you will see that your best Direction is shaded in red, with your other good but less significant directions in orange and yellow. Your bad Directions are not all bad, but they are Directions which you should try not to emphasize. They are coloured with the cooler shades of the spectrum and your worst Direction is coloured with the darkest colour. To find out the exact meanings of these Directions and how to modify or emphasize them see pages 50-51.

From a practical point of view what you should aim to do, if you have the option or you are building a house completely from scratch, is to position unimportant rooms like storerooms or toilets in your worst Directions, with important rooms like your bedroom in your best sectors. At any rate you should make great efforts not to locate your front door or main bedroom in the less auspicious sectors, especially the darkest coloured sector.

There are nine possible Kua numbers, with 5 having a different male/female interpretation. The warmest sectors are the most auspicious, while the coldest colours are the least auspicious.

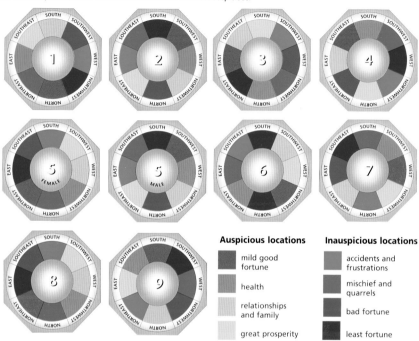

Auspicious locations

- mild good fortune
- health
- relationships and family
- great prosperity

Inauspicious locations

- accidents and frustrations
- mischief and quarrels
- bad fortune
- least fortune

The Chinese New Year

Before calculating your Kua number, you must first establish your year of birth according to the Chinese calendar. In practice this step only affects those who were born between 1st January and 20th February (if you were not born during this time, simply ignore this step). If you were born in this part of the year before the Chinese New Year (which varies from year to year) you should subtract 1 from your year of birth. For example someone born on 14th January 1966 will use 1965 for these calculations because the Chinese year 1965 did not end until 20th January 1966.

There is no simple rule for determining when the Chinese New Year occurs, except that in this century it occurs between 20th January and 20th February on the first New Moon of the year.

The Tung Shu or Chinese Almanac sells more than three million copies each year. It contains the date of the New Year.

5 The Feng-Shui of Your Home

Your **Front Door**

The front door to your house or flat is perhaps the most important feng-shui indicator and influence. It is like the mouth (or *kou*) of your dwelling and determines what *ch'i* is drawn into your home, whether positive or negative.

A circular doorway into a traditional Chinese garden, allowing entry of gently flowing ch'i.

The main door of your house should not open on to any obstruction like a high wall, a telegraph pole, a flyover or a source of 'secret arrows'. The main door should be solid and protective and not made of glass. It should not open into a narrow, dark or mean corridor, and it will be very constrictive to the entry of *ch'i* if the entrance hall has a beam in it.

Once the *ch'i* has entered the foyer, it circulates throughout the rest of the house. The arrangement of the corridors and stairs will then determine how the *ch'i* is distributed to the other rooms of the house. Ensure that corridors are well lit to keep the circulating *ch'i* 'bright'.

Internal doors should be examined because if they line up in straight lines or open directly on to another from the front to the rear of the house, they will encourage *sha ch'i* to move too rapidly through the home. To modify this, some kind of barrier should be put in place between them. For example, in a long straight corridor from the front to the back of the house, the placement of a small table with flowers on it causes *ch'i* to deflect and beneficially go around the table rather than cutting

straight through the room and escaping. Likewise internal doors directly opposite windows will encourage the loss of *ch'i*. Long corridors generally are a bad idea and are often the cause of problems in large offices, particularly those built in the 1950s and 1960s.

Interior door alignments are most important as they are the access routes for *ch'i* from one room to another. If for example three doors align so that *ch'i* can whistle from one room to another, this rapid passage should be slowed down by hanging a wind-chime in its path. Likewise, misaligned doors that indirectly face each other should have mirror strips added to the apparently narrower of the two, to even out the apparent width of the doors.

Favourable front door Directions

Ideally the front door should point in the most favourable Direction of the head of the household, and should not open on to an opposing blank wall or a major source of 'secret arrows', or on to the outer edge of a sharp bend in a road or watercourse. If any of the latter are unavoidable and cannot be blanked out, then maybe it is better to seal up the door and use the back door as your main house entrance, unless it is similarly afflicted.

Any of the Directions which are favourable to your Kua number (see pages 46-47) are good for your front door, but there is one special direction for each Kua number, called the *sheng ch'i* Direction (colour-coded yellow in the illustration on page 46), which is best of all. See the box for the best Direction for your specific Kua number.

If you haven't got the perfect front door Direction, don't worry too much. Any of the red or orange Directions for your Kua number will do almost as well.

The front door

Natal star or 'Kua number'	*Sheng ch'i* best front door Direction
1	Southeast
2	Northeast
3	South
4	North
5 (for a man)	Northeast
5 (for a woman)	Southwest
6	West
7	Northwest
8	Southwest
9	East

The view from your front door

Negative: roof lines generate 'secret arrows' but not as strongly as a satellite dish.

Negative: a satellite dish pointing directly at your front door is a strong source of 'secret arrows'.

Positive: a low wall in front of your door symbolizes the red phoenix.

Positive: a footstool or red phoenix formation in front of the door is good feng-shui. Ensure that any rocks used are smooth and don't form the shape of any potentially threatening creature.

Negative: the tree confronts the front door. This tree should ideally be screened by moving the gate entrance further along.

Negative: a church spire generates 'secret arrows'.

Negative: the sharp points of a saw-tooth fence create 'secret arrows'.

Positive: a pond to one side of your front door is beneficial, although you should be careful about its exact position. Ponds are powerful feng-shui and side effects have been known.

Positive: a curving path to your gate is much better feng-shui than a straight, 'cutting' path.

49

Feng-Shui

Pa Kua
in Your Home

The Pa Kua is the key to finding out which sectors of the house need stimulating in order to energize the various departments of your life.

Life aspirations

South: Recognition and fame

Southwest: Relationships and marriage

Southeast: Wealth

East: Family and health

West: Children

Northeast: Education and knowledge

North: Career

Northwest: Mentors/Helpful people

The whole house may be analyzed by placing the Pa Kua (see pages 32-33) over the ground-plan of the house. After which you need to analyze the attributions of each room in terms of the corresponding sector of the Pa Kua.

After examining the house as a whole, each individual room should have the Pa Kua placed over its plan to decide which quarter or corner of the room corresponds with which Direction and hence which sphere of activity.

Having calculated your Kua number, now is the time to use it. Your whole house can be divided into eight sectors marked out by the eight Trigrams arranged in the Later Heaven Sequence. Each Trigram is associated with a particular aspect of life, for example career, children, health and so on. They are sometimes referred to as 'life aspirations'. By checking the associations of each Trigram against your home, you can establish which rooms (or corners of a room) correspond to which aspiration.

The Trigrams and the family

Each Trigram also traditionally has a member of the family asociated with it, but these should be taken symbolically rather than literally:

Li:	Middle daughter	*K'an:*	Middle son
K'un:	Mother	*Ken:*	Youngest son
Tui:	Youngest daughter	*Chen:*	Eldest son
Ch'ien:	Father	*Sun:*	Eldest daughter

For example, the Trigram *K'un*, which is made of three Yin or broken lines is associated with the mother and marriage and relationships. As the Trigram *K'un* is attributed to the Southwest, this is the sector which should be stimulated to improve your marital or relationship prospects.

Workpoints

Orientate a Later Heaven Sequence Pa Kua (see opposite) on the floor in the centre of your home. Use a compass to make sure that the Trigram *Li* is pointed to the South. Then visually sight each of the cardinal points, then the four intercardinal points, marking down the room that corresponds to each sector in the Workpoint box.

A simple way of doing this is to draw a plan of your home, starting with the ground floor. Place the plan on a table so that it is aligned in the same Direction as your home, then place a compass on the plan, aligning the North-pointing needle with the North point on the compass. Use the compass to read off the basic Directions. Mark each room with a cardinal or intercardinal point. Using the illustration on the opposite page mark in the aspirations associated with each room.

If your home is complex enough to have several wings then each of these should be considered separately, with the most emphasis placed on the part of the structure which contains the front door.

When this has been completed, repeat the same process for your bedroom, noting down which walls or corners correspond to which aspirations, so that you will know which areas to stimulate.

Workpoint

Enter here the Directions of the rooms in your house:

Direction	Trigram	Aspiration	Which room
South	*Li*	Recognition and fame	
Southwest	*K'un*	Relationships/marriage	
West	*Tui*	Children	
Northwest	*Ch'ien*	Helpful people/patrons	
North	*K'an*	Career	
Northeast	*Ken*	Education and knowledge	
East	*Chen*	Family and health	
Southeast	*Sun*	Wealth	

Using the Pa Kua for room placement

When applying the Pa Kua to one of your rooms, make sure that the Trigram Li points to the South.

The doorway points in the Direction of the Li Trigram or Fire.

A sideboard should not be placed so as to create a corner in which ch'i can stagnate.

A window directly opposite the dining room table is not good feng-shui. It would be better if the chairs faced a wall rather than a window.

Furniture arranged in a square around a circular table is good feng-shui.

A plant has been placed in the corner to soften the flow of ch'i and to keep it circulating.

Rounded chairbacks do not create 'secret arrows'.

The centre of the room should be left clear and unobstructed.

N

Interior
Decorating

Mirrors as a whole are favoured decorative feng-shui cures.
They can act to mask an item which might otherwise generate
bad feng-shui. Ordinary mirrors can help move the *ch'i* around
your home, or if used with the Pa Kua symbols painted around
them, they can be used to deflect incoming 'secret arrows'
from outside the home.

Overhead beams press down on the smooth flow of *ch'i* and are 'burdens' which 'press down' on luck. Beams over a dining table are considered particularly bad. To alleviate this problem, you should spotlight them (enhancing Yang energy) to 'lift' the oppression. Alternatively you should hang a traditional wind 'cure', such as a pair of flutes, from them.

Square pillars, because they can send out 'cutting *ch'i*' in four Directions at once, need to be softened or disguised. One possible solution is to train a climbing plant up them. Alternatively they can be made to 'disappear' altogether by facing them with mirrors. Converting them into round columns is another option.

Colour

Colour plays an important part in both feng-shui and interior decoration within the home. The main purpose of adjusting the colours in a room is to balance the Yin and Yang elements, being careful to introduce at least 60% Yang for 40% Yin.

If an entire room is painted white and the furniture is cream, the overall effect may be very

Wind-chimes are useful for circulating ch'i and can be strategically placed to break up corridors or other straight alignments. Make sure that the pipes are hollow. A metal wind-chime can also be used to stimulate the Element Metal.

pleasing, but the Yin/Yang balance will not be satisfactory. Some darker Yin notes will have to be introduced to redress the balance.

Strong colours like red walls or furniture introduce Yang into the room. If it is necessary to introduce Yin highlights into a very male or Yang environment, then a selection of plants and flowers will soften the Yang and encourage the *ch'i* to meander and congregate.

Be careful that no wall colour confronts its own Direction; by that I mean that you should not paint a wall which faces West red because the symbolic colour of the West is red, nor should you paint a North-facing wall black, or a wall confronting a Wood Direction green and so on (see page 32 and the table opposite).

Enhancing Feng-Shui in your home

A wooden Pa Kua (see right) with a mirrored centre should only be used outside the home to deflect 'secret arrows' or other threatening structures.

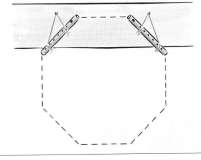

Inside the home feng-shui enhancers such as bamboo flutes may be hung strategically to enhance *ch'i* circulation. Symbolically, it is sometimes useful to combine the shape of the Pa Kua by physically hanging a pair of bamboo flutes so that they form two of the slanting sides of an imaginary octagon (see drawing).

Colour can be provided more permanently by paint, or temporarily by coloured light bulbs which are useful to illuminate specific sectors. For example, your career could be stimulated by illuminating the North quarter with a blue bulb as the Element Water is associated in feng-shui with either dark blue or black.

Bamboo flutes are wind (or feng) instruments. They can be used to ease the flow of ch'i around obstructions like overhead beams.

Colour around the home

The basic Chinese interpretation of colour is symbolic. Each colour is also attributed to one of the five Elements. The strongest feng-shui colours are red, green and gold and they are used in the painting of the Pa Kua and many other Chinese decorations.

Red for happiness/festivity (Fire)

Green for peace and eternity, posterity and harmony (Wood)

White for peace, purity and sometimes mourning (Metal)

Gold for royalty, strength and wealth (also Metal)

Silver represents Metal

Yellow for gaiety (Earth)

Black for calamity (Water)

Blue for Heaven (dark blue also represents Water)

6   Your Rooms and Your Garden

Your **Living** *and* **Dining** *Room*

The living room and dining room, being the social centres of the house, should be designed with unity in mind. More than in any other room in the house, the flow of *ch'i* must be as uninterrupted as possible.

Good luck and good health are often symbolized by Chinese vases. The Dragon decoration symbolizes the flow of ch'i *through the earth.*

Traditionally, the best arrangement for living room furniture is one in which there are no sharp protuberances. Try to avoid incomplete L-shaped arrangements of chairs and sofas, as well as L-shaped rooms and L-shaped houses.

The flow of *ch'i* through the room must be unhindered, with a smooth exit, perhaps through a second door. Furniture may be arranged in circular, square or octagonal (Pa Kua-shaped) groupings in the middle of the floor. Arrange the furniture, especially chairs and the sofa, so that their backs do not face the doorway. Try to create a focus point.

Particular attention should be paid to furniture that is left out of these groupings and is lined up along the wall. Such items should be checked to ensure that they do not generate their own minor 'secret arrows' through being aligned with an open door, or with some part of the centre grouping. Corners should be occupied by enlivening items such as plants (only in the appropriate corner such as the Southwest) with a view to preventing the stagnation of *ch'i*.

Each window and door should be considered according to the direction of the inflowing *ch'i*. The *ch'i* should follow the lines of the furnishings in a spiral from room to room before it exhausts itself. The living room should not be cut off from the rest of the house in such a way that it can become a repository for stagnant *ch'i*. The converse of this is also true: a living room with too many doors is not only draughty but is liable to be a disperser of *ch'i*.

It should also be easy to move around the living room without bumping into the corners of protruding furniture, for the flow of *ch'i* is very much like the movements of a dancer who will not perform well on a cluttered stage.

Dining rooms

If possible all dining chairs should back on to a wall rather than in the direction of a doorway. Neither the dining table nor any of the chairs should be positioned under an overhead beam. If this is unavoidable, then a false ceiling might be the best answer to this problem.

Living rooms with good and bad Feng-Shui

Some bad points

• Too many **dark colours** and heavy furniture will effect the Yin/Yang harmony. A few lighter colours should be introduced to redress the balance.

• **Overhead beams** press down on the smooth flow of *ch'i* and are 'burdens' on posterity. Two bamboo flutes hung at 45° angles would conduct *ch'i* downwards and away from the area of congestion.

• A living room with too many **doorways** is draughty and also disperses positive *ch'i*.

• **Furniture** should be arranged around a central focal point and should not point towards a doorway.

Some good points

• **Furniture** should be arranged in a circular, square or octagonal grouping.
• **Round tables** are good feng-shui as positive *ch'i* is allowed to circulate.
• **Plants** soften the Yang and encourage positive *ch'i* to congregate and meander.
• Lots of **light** in a room promotes good energy.

Your **Bedroom**

The bedroom is perhaps the most significant room to examine after the positioning of the front door. After all, we spend about a third of our lives in our bedroom and so its feng-shui characteristics are obviously going to affect us deeply.

Examples of bad feng-shui in the bedroom: a mirror directly reflecting the bed will contribute to disturbed nights; the metal bed frame will create 'secret arrows' aimed at the occupants; an overhanging and therefore threatening pair of pictures above the bed will subconsciously disturb the occupants; a heavy chandelier hanging directly above the bed will press down upon the occupants.

The location of the bedroom within the house is most important. The *Nien Yen* sector is the ideal location in the house for your bedroom (see table). *Nien Yen* means 'longevity with descendants' and has a positive influence upon marital happiness. The *Nien Yen* sector is sand-coloured on page 47.

The position of your bed

Paying attention to the direction in which we sleep is one of the most important aspects of the layout of the bedroom. Many people have strong feelings about the direction in which they sleep, some finding one direction comfortable, and others finding the same direction uncomfortable and the apparent cause of restless nights.

The head of your bed should be pointed in one of your four best Directions as determined by your Kua number, especially your *Nien Yen* direction (see table). The bed direction can affect all sorts of things including career, relationship and marriage fortune.

Try to sleep with the head of the bed placed against a wall for support as this reinforces your sense of security. Headboards likewise help with this feeling of support in the same way that a mountain range situated behind a house gives it support.

Bad feng-shui for the bedroom

There are a few basic rules which should not be broken, the main one being that you should not sleep with your head pointed towards the door of the bedroom. This is because consciously or subconsciously there will always be a feeling of uneasiness about who might be entering the room if they cannot immediately be seen. Make sure that you do not face the open door of an en-suite bathroom as the stagnant water-produced *ch'i* from here will weaken your *ch'i* accumulation.

Mirrors should be placed where they cannot be seen from the bed. The same applies to mirror tiles because they 'break up' the image, and therefore the relationship, reflected in them.

The bedroom should have only one entrance, so that the sleeper can absorb the accumulating *ch'i* rather than have it disperse rapidly out through a second doorway. The door of the bedroom should not open on to a stairwell or a kitchen as an undesirable rush of energy will come in through the door.

The bedroom should never be built over an empty space, a storeroom or a garage because it creates a *ch'i* vacuum underneath and adversely affects the occupants.

It is strongly recommended that you do not sleep in a room with an overhead beam, especially one that passes over the bed itself. The same rule applies to sloping, loft or A-frame ceilings which trap negative *ch'i* and pose a subconscious threat.

The Bedroom

Natal star or 'Kua number'	*Nien Yen* or main bedroom Directions
1	South
2	Northwest
3	Southeast
4	East
5 (for a man)	Northwest
5 (for a woman)	West
6	Southwest
7	Northeast
8	West
9	North

Bedroom Feng-Shui

Some bad points

This bed is very badly positioned, being directly in line with the doorway, the door itself, as well as the window. *Ch'i* will flow rapidly through the door, across the bed and out of the window. In addition the head of the bed is not supported by a solid backing wall.

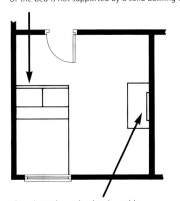

The mirror above the dressing table strikes directly at the bed and will cause sleepless nights.

After Feng-Shui corrections

A plant has been placed just inside the door to modify the flow of *ch'i* entering the room.

A rounded dressing table helps to deflect the direct flow of *ch'i* from the open door towards the window.

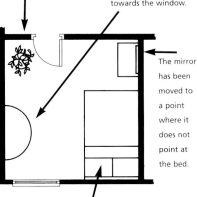

The mirror has been moved to a point where it does not point at the bed.

The head of the bed is now supported by the wall and the occupants can immediately see anyone entering through the door.

Your **Bathroom** and Toilet

The location of your bathroom is not particularly critical, although the presence of running water in this room affects the water or *shui* balance of the house. Far more critical is the location of your toilet.

The toilet often tends to be in, or adjacent to, the bathroom and because it is from this room that water, and hence *ch'i*, is regularly flushed away, the location is all-important. Even within a bathroom, toilets should if possible be aligned away from the bathroom door or hidden behind a half wall.

The position of the toilet should be carefully considered because the constant flushing of water disturbs the balance of ch'i in its vicinity. Here the householder has placed a screen in such a way that the toilet is not directly visible to anyone entering the room.

From a feng-shui point of view, whatever qualities are attributed to this sector will tend to get symbolically 'flushed away' because the toilet's watery connections act as a drain on *ch'i* accumulation. Toilets are also a strong generator of excess Yin and *sha ch'i*.

Accordingly, feng-shui practitioners always recommend that toilets are as unobtrusive as possible. Therefore the first feng-shui rule with regard to the toilet is always keep it closed: both the lid and the door. Put a spring-closer on the door if you can, so that it closes even if you forget.

A toilet should not face directly towards the main entrance of a house. Also a ventilated lobby is desirable between the toilet and the rest of the house. However, if your toilet is located in one of your most inauspicious Directions (see page 47), then the toilet will symbolically contribute to flushing away these bad influences. Armed with your Kua number, you can check if your toilet is well located (see table).

Bad toilet locations
The worst location for a toilet would be the places listed on pages 48-49 as your ideal front door location. A toilet located in the Southeast, the wealth corner of the house, will certainly flush away your wealth almost as fast as it is created. If it is located in the Southwest corner of the house, then marital problems are likely. Positioning the toilet in the North will delay your career prospects.

The Toilet	
Natal star or 'Kua number'	**Best toilet Directions**
1	Southwest, Northwest, Northeast
2	North, Southeast, South
3	West, Northwest, Northeast
4	Southwest, West, Northeast
5 (for a man)	North, Southeast, South
5 (for a woman)	North, East, Southeast
6	North, East, South
7	East, Southeast, South
8	North, East, Southeast
9	Southwest, West, Northwest

Flushing the toilet bowl is seen symbolically as flushing away accumulated water and therefore accumulated wealth.

Your **Kitchen**

The kitchen is one of the most important rooms in the house and it is associated with the nourishment and health of the family. If the kitchen is located in an inappropriate position, then illness and loss of livelihood can strike the occupants. The kitchen location also has health implications.

In many countries the kitchen is much more the social centre of the house than any other room. According to feng-shui principles, the kitchen door must be shielded away from direct access from the front door and should be in a position where the cook will not have his/her back to the door for too much of the time.

The structure of your kitchen is important. It should have a well-proportioned entrance door which allows the entry of *ch'i* and have a regular shape. The various facilities in a kitchen are easily assigned to their Elements. For example, the stove or cooker is obviously a Fire item, while the fridge and sink are both attributed to Water. Ideally the Fire of the cooker should not be opposite and in confrontation with either of the Water facilities (the fridge and sink). The Direction that the cooker faces is the most important factor. It must not directly

Although superficially appealing, this galley kitchen has some serious feng-shui drawbacks. First there is an Element conflict between the Water of the sink and the opposing Fire of the stove. The positioning of the doors and windows means that 'secret arrows' can strike directly into the kitchen which should normally be the most protected part of the home.

face either the back or front doors, otherwise valuable *ch'i* will be lost. If the kitchen is not on the ground floor, then this is less of a problem.

There is one special Direction, called the *T'ien Yi* direction, which is the best location in the house for your kitchen. If you can't simply re-orientate your kitchen, and few of us can, try to organize it so that the mouth of your stove, or at least the mouth of your microwave, points in this Direction. The importance of the oven mouth is that this provides nourishment to the family and therefore represents health and wealth. Depending upon your Kua number, the best Directions are given in the table. Make sure that your oven mouth does not face any of your inauspicious Directions (see pages 46–47).

The introduction of green into the kitchen, symbolizing Wood, helps to support both the Fire and Water Elements that make up the kitchen. The kitchen symbolizes everything from wealth to family bonds. As the rapid through movement of *ch'i* is

bad feng-shui, try not to have windows or second doorways in line with the main door. Where the kitchen is part of the dining room, as in a studio flat, provide a demarcation line between the two.

The Kitchen

Natal star or 'Kua number'	*T'ien Yi* best oven Direction
1	East
2	West
3	North
4	South
5 (for a man)	West
5 (for a woman)	Northwest
6	Northeast
7	Southwest
8	Northwest
9	Southeast

Kitchen Feng-Shui

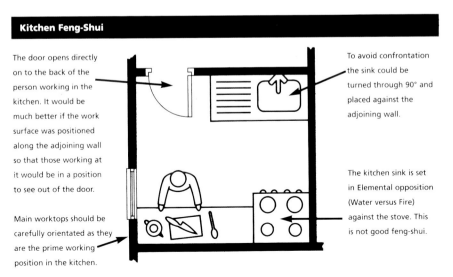

The door opens directly on to the back of the person working in the kitchen. It would be much better if the work surface was positioned along the adjoining wall so that those working at it would be in a position to see out of the door.

Main worktops should be carefully orientated as they are the prime working position in the kitchen.

To avoid confrontation the sink could be turned through 90° and placed against the adjoining wall.

The kitchen sink is set in Elemental opposition (Water versus Fire) against the stove. This is not good feng-shui.

Your **Garden**

In the garden, you generally have much greater freedom to change things and configure your own feng-shui environment. The essence of enhancing feng-shui is to balance the Yin and the Yang in the garden so that *ch'i* is encouraged to flow in a lazy, meandering fashion and to accumulate. Thus the presence of soft Yin foliage can be countered with the Yang of polished stones or boulders.

This garden shows a naturalistic approach with curved paths, a mature pond and well-screened peripheral boundaries.

Designing your garden

The design of the garden should not be flat and lifeless or a basic rectangular shape where every part can be seen immediately upon entering the garden. If your garden is laid out in a rectangular fashion, then maybe the introduction of a little imagination to give it more natural lines could work wonders. Try to introduce curving paths and planting patterns which lead the eye into the middle distance, but don't reveal the whole garden. Both these objectives can be achieved with a curving path apparently disappearing behind a screen of plants.

Walls and fences

These can either let in or keep out surrounding feng-shui influences. They are very important as screens to block 'secret arrows'. So first of all walk carefully around your garden noting what you can see over the fences from every part of the garden. You should add additional trellis work to the top of fences to block out views of 'cutting' shapes, such as the intrusive lines of telegraph poles. By growing a vine over the trellis you soften or remove the cutting *ch'i* generated by that shape. Where the view is beneficial, the opposite holds true, and often a good outlook can be brought into your garden by constructing round 'portholes' in the walls if they are made of brick or simply lowering the height of a fence.

Try to encourage or locate strongly growing plants next to your walls and fences: this helps to modify the stark Yangness of the fence with the soft Yin of the foliage.

Paths and garden edging

These are important elements in the overall feng-shui environment of the garden. Try to visualize these as if they were streams and see where their natural flow leads. If garden edging runs in straight lines alongside rectangular beds, then this will create 'secret arrows' and become a source of undesirable *sha*. If both paths and edging are laid out in curves they can take the place of streams and actually help to accumulate *ch'i*.

Garden edging performs a similar task in conducting *ch'i*. If edging is to conduct the flow of *ch'i* properly, it is important that loose earth or plants must not be prevented from covering the edging or blurring its definition.

A well-planned garden

• The **path** flows in a curved, meandering fashion through the garden, much like a stream.

• **Plants** cloak the harsh fence lines and the pond helps to accumulate *ch'i*. Advanced feng-shui has much to say about the exact positioning of ponds and watercourses.

• The **round table** and round-backed chairs deflect *sha ch'i*.

• The large stone **ornament** introduces a touch of Yang to the garden to balance the Yin foliage and plants.

63

Glossary

cardinal points	North, South, East, West
ch'i	the vital energy of the universe, or 'cosmic breath'
compass school	the Fukien school of feng-shui which uses the feng-shui compass to diagnose ch'i flows. Early master was Wang Chih (circa 960 AD)
Direction	one of the 24 compass Directions, such as tzu in the North
Earlier Heaven Sequence	a circular arrangement of the Eight Trigrams such that the Trigram Ch'ien is in the South. Used on defensive Pa Kua and for burial site feng-shui
Elements	the five Chinese Elements: Water, Fire, Wood, Earth, Metal
fang-shih	master of Taoist magic
feng	wind
feng sha	a noxious ch'i-destroying wind
feng-shui	the Chinese system of maximizing the accumulation of ch'i to improve the quality of life, literally 'wind and water'
feng-shui hsien-sheng	a practitioner of feng-shui
form school	feng-shui practice common in Kiangsi which uses the form of the surrounding landscape to determine the location of the ch'i flow
geomancy	a European and African form of earth-divining totally unrelated to feng-shui. The early missionaries in China in the 1870s incorrectly used 'geomancy' as a translation of feng-shui
hexagram	the 64 figures formed by placing one Trigram on top of another in all their possible permutations. A figure with eight lines, either broken or unbroken
hsing	one of the five Chinese Elements, Water, Fire, Wood, Earth, Metal

hsiu	constellations
I Ching	the Chinese Classic of Changes, a philosophical and divinatory book based on the 64 hexagrams
intercardinal points	Northeast, Northwest, Southeast, Southwest
kua	see Trigram (kua in Chinese)
Later Heaven Sequence	a circular arrangement of the eight Trigrams such that the Trigram Li is in the South. Used for feng-shui of houses and cities
lo p'an	the feng-shui compass
lo shu	the magic square with nine chambers, whose numbers add up to fifteen in any direction, connected with the Later Heaven Sequence of Trigrams
Pa Kua	the eight-sided or circular arrangement of the eight Trigrams
'secret arrow'	a ch'i-destroying alignment of an adjacent road, property, etc.
sector	one of the cardinal or intercardinal points, i.e. North, South, East, West, Northeast, Northwest, Southeast, Southwest
sha or sha ch'i	stagnant ch'i
shui	water
t'ai-chi	the great Absolute from which everything else came
Taoism	a Chinese religious and mystical belief concerned with Tao and the way of flow and harmony
t'ien	heaven
Trigram	eight figures made up of three Yang (whole) or Yin (broken) lines
tzu	due North (and other meanings)
Yang	male active energy, the opposite of Yin
Yang Yun-Sung	early master of the Form School of feng-shui (circa 888 AD)
Yin	female passive energy, the opposite of Yang